KV-322-955

How it is made

Oil Rigs

Text   Michael Lynch
Design   Arthur Lockwood

Contents

ff
faber and faber in association with Threshold Books

What is an oil rig?

For people outside the oil business the term 'oil rig' is generally applied to the complex structure – on land or sea – which drills for oil. To be accurate, the rig is the vessel which searches for oil at sea – the **exploration rig**. However, because the early equipment which oilmen used was known as a rig, the term now refers to many structures in the oil-producing industry – particularly to the oil platform, that appears so regularly on news programmes about the North Sea and other offshore oil fields.

Basically, an exploration rig is a mobile structure which is used for drilling holes in the hope of locating oil. **Oil**, or **production, platforms**, are fixed structures installed at an oil field to produce oil once it has been found.

The title of this book covers both of these structures, but within the book the term 'oil rig' will be used only to refer to an **exploration rig**.

On land, exploration can be carried out by using a simple wooden tower, or **derrick**. At sea, drilling is far more difficult, and a number of structures are available. The type of rig to be used will depend very much on the depth of the water and the local weather conditions.

Whichever rig is chosen, its basic purpose is to provide a stable platform designed to hold all the necessary drilling equipment. The ability to move quickly to another area for further drilling may also be important.

Early attempts to drill offshore began in the 1920s in the swamps of Louisiana in the United States, and in shallow lakes such as Lake Erie in Canada and Lake Maracaibo in Venezuela. These early efforts were made from wooden platforms standing on the sea bed, but in modern offshore drilling the latest technological knowledge and equipment are needed.

The main factors which have to be taken into account are the depth of water, the weather prospects, and the particular sea bed conditions. Offshore drilling platforms must accommodate the drilling crew, the derrick, and drilling machines, as well as a helicopter deck and other items.

A jack-up barge – complete with helicopter deck – drilling a well in the North Sea.

ue

MATTHEW BOULTON TECHNICAL COLLEGE, BIRMINGHAM

LIBRARY

P28852

Classification No.	Book No.
622.328 LYN	33013 ✓

BOOKS MUST BE RETURNED OR RENEWED ON OR BEFORE THE LAST DATE STAMPED BELOW

23. MAR 1990

12. NOV 90

08. NOV 94

29. NOV 94

MAR 95

29. JUN 95

019541

MATTHEW BOULTON
TECHNICAL COLLEGE
COLLEGE LIBRARY

33013

622·328

There are three main types of offshore oil rig:

1 Jack-up barge (below left)

This rig is a barge which carries three, four or more huge legs. The barge is towed to the area where drilling is to take place, with the legs above the water. Once the barge is in position, the legs are lowered until they touch the sea bed. The barge itself is then jacked-up above the surface of the waves. The disadvantage of the jack-up barge is that at present it can be used only at water depths of 100 metres (328 feet) or less.

2 Drill ship (above)

The drill ship was invented to cope with deeper waters (down to 1200 metres, or 3937 feet). It is specially designed to incorporate drilling equipment, including a derrick. Drilling is carried out through a hole in the bottom of the vessel. The major advantage of this type of rig over the jack-up barge is that it can move under its own power to a new drilling site. Its main *dis*advantage is that, like any other ship, it is susceptible to the movement of wind and sea, which means that drilling must often be stopped until the weather clears. The rigs are therefore better suited to the calmer waters of the Far East.

3 Semi-submersible (right)

These huge structures, the latest and most spectacular development in offshore exploration, stand on giant buoyancy tanks floating below the surface of the water. As well as keeping the rigs afloat, the tanks also keep them steady, so that drilling can be carried out in deep waters and in fairly heavy seas.

In the early days the semi-submersibles were towed to the drilling area and anchored to the sea bed. Today they are held in position by motors operated by computer. The constant firing of the motors keeps the rig in one place. At present it is the semi-submersibles which carry out much of the exploration in the North Sea. Once oil is discovered, the rigs move on, and the wells are drilled from a production platform.

In this dry dock the four columns are being constructed which support the deck structure of a semi-submersible.

When the deck is complete the familiar derrick is installed.

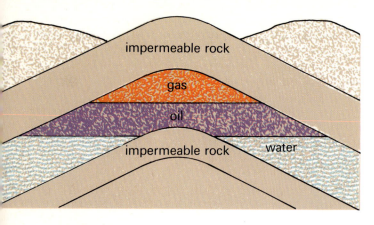

Anticlines

The anticlinal trap is the simplest and commonest form. In an anticline a porous reservoir rock is sealed above by a fine grained, relatively impermeable bed such as clay, shale or salt. The structure is in the form of a dome that forms a closed space in which oil can accumulate.

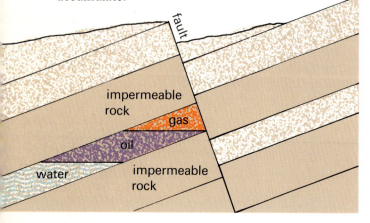

Faults

Fault traps are also common. Again, there must be a porous reservoir rock sealed above by an impermeable layer. But the real trap is provided by the fault in the rocks which itself forms a barrier to prevent the oil escaping round it.

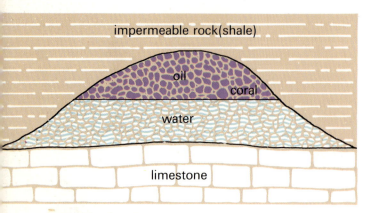

Stratigraphic traps

Stratigraphic traps also require a porous reservoir rock and impermeable seal.

There are three forms of oil accumulations. These are known as anticlinal, fault, and stratigraphic traps. About 80–90 per cent of the known petroleum reserves are found in either anticlines or faults.

Finding the oil

The first successful oil well was drilled in the United States in 1859. An American (known as 'Colonel' Drake) was drilling for brine, or salt, in Pennsylvania when he unexpectedly struck oil. In next to no time the wooden towers of the first rigs had sprung up all over the area, and hundreds of would-be oilmen had arrived, hoping to make their fortune.

At that time the only product refined from crude oil was kerosine, which was used as fuel for paraffin lamps. The 'waste' material was thrown away, as there was no use for it. Fifty years were to elapse before the invention of the internal combustion engine, which provided a ready market for the new oil industry.

The early wells were drilled on land, to quite shallow depths. Later, as technology improved, it became possible to dig down deeper and deeper into the earth – both on land and at sea. Knowing where to drill is not easy. The earliest oil-strikes often happened by chance, as there is no known way of locating crude oil directly. The oilman does not have recourse to a simple rod like that used by a water diviner. Clues to the presence of oil lie in certain types of rock.

Today most scientists believe that crude oil had its origins in organic waste. In prehistoric times the seas were teeming with microscopic creatures, such as plankton, many of which were carried along by the sand and mud of rivers. When these creatures died they sank to the sea bed and, with other dead animals and decaying plants, formed waste matter which was buried in the thick layers of gravel and sediment. Gradually the layers solidified into sandstone and limestone rock, which in time became distorted by movements in the earth's crust. Some parts of the earth which were once under the sea were pushed up above sea level, to form dry land.

During a period lasting millions of years, the pressure of the layers of rock, together with heat and the action of bacteria, created crude oil. The oil is found in the minute spaces within the rock itself, and it is for these areas of sedimentary rock that geologists search the earth's surface. The main areas are sedimentary basins which were once under the sea, but which are not flat. To find out if oil exists, a bore-hole is drilled. A bore-hole is an exploratory attempt to discover oil or gas. If oil or gas is present, the bore-hole is widened and strengthened and becomes a well.

Another means of detection used is by **seismic survey,** in which sound waves – such as those caused by an explosion on the earth's surface – are 'bounced' off underground rocks. By analysing the echoes recorded, geologists can construct a 'profile' of the rocks deep down in the earth. But even when the geologist finds the right rock structure, there is still no way of knowing if oil is present until a bore-hole is dug. As drilling is extremely expensive, the oilmen have to be pretty sure that there is a likelihood of oil being found before they begin to drill.

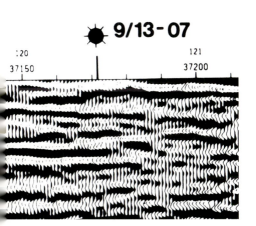

A small part of a print-out from a seismic survey.

A charge is detonated from the survey vessel. The resulting shock waves 'bounce back' from the layers of rock and give geologists a 'picture' of the internal structure. These shock waves are picked up on a series of receivers or geophones towed behind the ship.

An offshore seismic survey. A geologist checks the firing of charges on board a survey vessel.

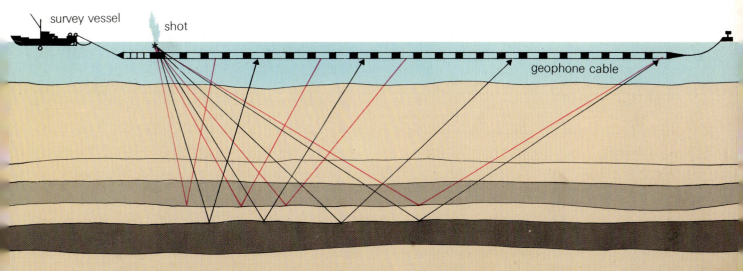

Drilling methods

Since the beginning of time, mankind's most basic need has been for water. When it cannot be found on the earth's surface, in lakes and rivers, it has to be dug out. Throughout the centuries, in most hot, dry areas this has been done by hand.

In ancient China, however, a more efficient method was developed. A large, pointed stone was suspended on a rope over a springboard. Men then jumped on and off the springboard, causing it to jerk the stone up and down. Each time that the stone fell, it dug down into the earth, enabling the well to be 'drilled' without causing danger to the digger. Salt, or brine, wells were drilled to a depth of over 300 metres (984 feet) by the Chinese, who cased the sides of the wells with bamboo.

In the 19th century the first attempts by Europeans at digging for crude oil and gas were on roughly the same principle as those used long ago by the Chinese, but the stone was replaced by a chisel-shaped iron instrument, or **bit**. It drilled narrow wells, only about 10 centimetres (4 inches) in diameter, and seldom reaching down deeper than 100 metres (328 feet). This method of drilling pulverised the soil and soft rock and was known as the **percussion system**.

The next significant development came with the invention of the steam engine, which provided much greater power for the bit. A wooden derrick was built above the well, and a length of steel wire (replacing the rope) was suspended from the top of the tower. The steam engine was used to work a crank which hoisted the drill-bit to the top of the tower. The bit was then released, and it hit the earth with considerable force, thus digging wider and deeper wells. The use of wire speeded up the whole process, since it did not snap, as rope often did. Iron casing was used to protect the sides of the well, and the derrick enabled it to be hoisted into position and pushed into the well far more easily than before.

By the 1930s this system of drilling – called the **cable-tool system** – was well established, but although it was a great improvement on earlier drilling methods it still had its disadvantages. The main problem was what happened when the oil or gas was actually struck. If the liquid or gas was under pressure it sprayed

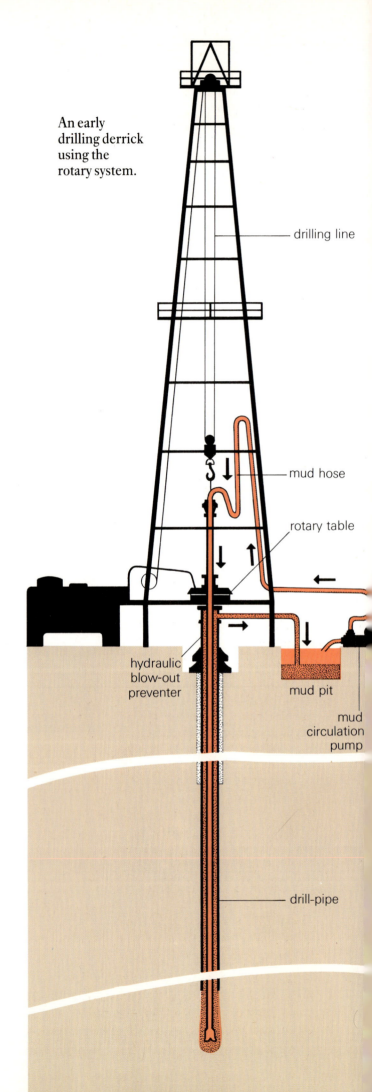

An early drilling derrick using the rotary system.

drilling line

mud hose

rotary table

hydraulic blow-out preventer

mud pit

mud circulation pump

drill-pipe

out of the well with uncontrollable force. These **gushers**, as they were called, were dangerous, often causing fires which raged for weeks.

The next invention, later on in the 1930s, was the **rotary system**. Instead of a heavy weight punching a hole in the ground, a rotating bit was used – on the same principle as a power drill • making a hole in metal or wood.

The bit was attached to a length of piping instead of to a steel wire and was passed through a circular steel table positioned on the ground above the well. A steam engine rotated the table, which in turn rotated the drill-pipe. Then the hook from which the drill-pipe hung was lowered so that the drill-pipe could bore into the earth.

As the bit dug deeper and deeper, more lengths of piping (stored in the derrick) were added at the top. To provide additional weight, much heavier lengths of drill-pipe were positioned immediately above the bit, forcing it to bite further down into the rock, thus digging deeper wells. To overcome the problems of gushers, a series of valves were fitted over the well which could be shut off if oil or gas surged up under pressure. In modern wells these **blow-out preventers** make gushers virtually a thing of the past.

The drilling process

A **drill-bit** is fixed to lengths of drill-pipe and rotated by a motor. The bit bores a hole deep into the earth. As it goes through rock it becomes extremely hot and has to be cooled by pumping a substance called 'drilling-mud' down through the drill-pipe. The mud flows out of holes in the drill-bit itself and then moves upwards on the outer side of the drill-pipe.

Drilling-mud is a chemical mixture which has several useful functions. Not only does it cool the bit, it also lubricates it to make the drilling easier. In addition it carries rocky fragments upwards to the surface where they can be analysed by geologists. Finally it acts as an enormous bung, providing a check against an uprush of oil, water or gas, under pressure.

As well as the rotary drill, another method is by **turbo-drilling**, in which a turbine is placed just above the bit and is driven by a current of drilling-mud forced down the bore-hole under pressure. An important advantage of turbo-drilling is that it does not waste energy, as the turbine drives the bit which is right next to it. In rotary drilling the rotating table is often thousands of feet away from the rotating drill-bit.

An oilman checks the enormous drill-bit required to drill the wells. Above the main bit are three smaller bits which help widen the hole.

Here is a giant blow-out preventer stack on board a drilling rig. This complex set of values helps prevent uncontrolled oil bursting out of the well.

Exploration rigs

In the early 1970s the beginning of the world economic recession, following the sudden and dramatic rise in oil prices, was a serious setback to shipping companies. Their need for new ships became almost non-existent, so the shipyards had to look for alternative business. For many of them, building offshore structures for oil companies was a practical solution.

Until this time, exploration rigs had been built mainly in Norway and Japan. Then in 1972 Scott Lithgow Ltd at Govan in Scotland was awarded an order for a **'dynamically positioned' drillship** – the 'Ben Ocean Lancer'. Throughout the 1970s valuable knowledge and experience were gained and the shipyards began to build semi-submersible drilling rigs on a large scale.

To do its job efficiently a drilling rig must fulfil certain essential requirements. The most important is that it should be stable and buoyant, so that it can operate in rough seas; this is achieved with large steel buoyancy tanks, or **pontoons**. Secondly, it must have a large deck

rotary table

guide lines

marine riser

flexible control cables

blow-out preventer

anchor

drill-pipe

cement

This diagram shows an exploration rig positioned over the well. The drill-pipes will stretch for many thousands of feet.

mud

bit

A view from the underside of a drilling rig. Clearly visible is the main riser which houses the lengths of drill-pipe connected to the bit.

area. This in turn is supported by columns, which rest on the pontoons. Columns and pontoons (which are all sub-divided, to limit any flooding should there be an accident) can weigh up to 4,000 tonnes, with the deck structure weighing as much again.

On top of all this weight is the equipment needed for the drilling operations. The most familiar part of the structure is the derrick, which may be as much as 70 metres (230 feet) high. Other important parts are the **rotary drill equipment**; the **riser system** which brings the oil up to the surface; and **blow-out preventers** to stop uncontrolled surges of oil. Among many other pieces of equipment are the numerous lengths of drill-pipe, the pipe racks, cranes, lifeboats, generators, helicopter deck, and so on. The rig must also carry fuel oil, drill-water, and mud tanks.

The pontoons are built in huge covered halls, and when complete are moved out to twin dry docks, where the columns are constructed. Once the columns are in place, the building of the deck structure can begin. The various deck modules are built in the building halls, ready for installation. Other parts of the yard include large steel production shops to produce the miles of pipework required.

Once completed in the dry docks, the submersible rig – a cross between a ship and a land-based drilling structure – is floated out and towed to its drilling position where it will drill holes as far down as 2,000 metres (6,562 feet) in the sea bed.

Pontoons which support the columns which in turn hold the deck structure of a drilling rig are constructed in huge covered halls.

Welding is a key skill in the construction of rigs and platforms.

Steel platforms

accommodation

drilling

production

deck support frame

jacket

sea bed piles

The first offshore platform to be positioned out of sight of land was made of steel. It was built in the late 1940s in the Gulf of Mexico.

The main purpose of steel platforms is to provide a stable structure from which drilling can be carried out. The platforms can be either gravity structures or piled structures. A **gravity structure** is cheaper, as it merely sits on the sea bed and is kept in position by its own weight.

A deck support frame is positioned on top of the jacket to hold the deck modules.

Such platforms have been used off the west coast of Africa. **Piled structures** are held in place by a series of steel piles, or posts, which are driven through the base of the platform and secured to the sea bed.

A steel platform consists of several parts. Starting from the bottom, there is the **pile foundation**; next comes the **steel substructure** or **jacket**, which is largely underwater; on top of this is the **deck support frame**, which will be just above the waves; and finally there is the **platform** itself, with all its facilities.

Steel platforms are built on their sides, in specially designed graving docks on the shore. The jacket, which is the basic structure, is made up of a great number of tubular steel units welded together, which have to support all the facilities needed for drilling wells and for producing oil or gas. Their enormous weight has to be transferred through the steel crosspieces to the sea floor and into the piles. Construction of the jacket can take up to twenty-four months.

Steel platforms are made up of the lower 'jacket' and deck support frame on which the whole structure stands, and the upper 'deck' which houses accommodation, drilling and production facilities.

The search for oil has extended to deeper and deeper waters, necessitating different construction techniques.

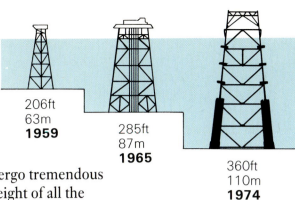

206ft
63m
1959

285ft
87m
1965

360ft
110m
1974

1000+ft
305m
1980

An oil platform has to undergo tremendous stresses: not only from the weight of all the equipment that it carries but from the environment in which it stands. The North Sea is a particularly harsh area, and the platform must be capable of remaining stable when battered by stormy seas and powerful winds. The designers must also take into account the conditions of the sea bed: such as undercurrents which can scour away the area around the platform base, and the problems of corrosion. From the data collected on these potential problems, decisions are made as to how many piles are needed and how they can best be installed. If, for example, the sea bed is made up of hard rock, holes may have to be pre-drilled and the piles inserted into them. In softer soil the piles can be hammered in. In either case the job has to be finished off with a cement **grouting** to hold the piles in position.

Special test tanks are used to examine the effects of weather by simulating extreme storm waves on models of the jacket structures; the results are then analysed by computer. By studying records of previous weather conditions specialists can predict the likely stresses and strains that a platform will have to undergo over the next 20 years.

And it is not just the unusual storm wave – which may occur only once in 100 years – that has to be taken into account. The possible effect of continual battering of the platform by much smaller waves, which can cause metal fatigue, also has to be studied. By using the very latest computer techniques the oil companies can bring together all these important data at the design stage.

MATTHEW BOULTON
TECHNICAL COLLEGE
COLLEGE LIBRARY

Safety is paramount in drilling operations. Here, a small-scale model of the hull of a semi-submersible undergoes stringent testing in a water tank.

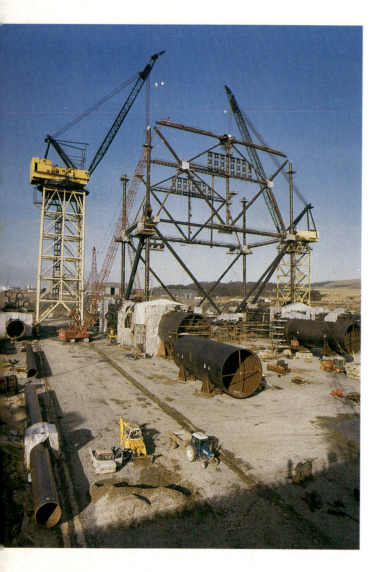

One of the most crucial stages in the construction of the jacket is the welding of the steel tubes, which requires the highest standard of workmanship. Once the tubes are completed, the welds are X-ray and ultra-sonic tested.

The **main structural members** are made from steel plate, which is rolled into tubes of the required size. The **secondary parts** of the platform are constructed elsewhere from ready-made tubular steel and brought to the site. Other components such as handrails, walk-ways and casings are also constructed elsewhere, generally from milder steel, as they do not have to bear loads.

A typical steel production platform is the one commissioned in 1973 by Mobil for its Beryl B oil field in the North Sea. The jacket itself is 130 metres (427 feet) high, and has eight legs, three of which will ultimately be used for the storage of drilling water and diesel fuel. At launch it weighed 14,000 tonnes.

Left: The beginning of a steel platform. The tractor and JCB in the foreground give some indication of scale. The jacket is constructed on its side in a dry dock which later will be flooded.

Below: Underneath the giant network of tubular steel pipes which form one side of the jacket.

The jacket nears completion. Notice how close the sea water is. The wall holding back the sea will be removed when the dock is flooded. Notice also the double-decker bus in the foreground, positioned to illustrate the size of the jacket.

This is a pile cluster being towed to the dry dock. Manufactured elsewhere, the pile clusters are welded to the base of the jacket. Ultimately the piles – which fix the platform to the sea bed – will pass through the 9 holes round the perimeter.

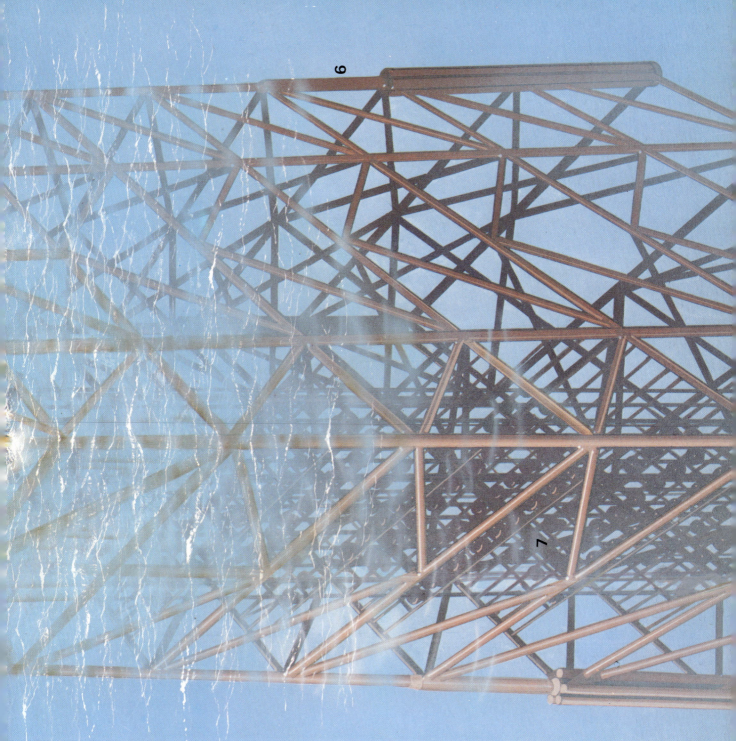

6

7

This steel jacket is 151 metres (495 ft) tall, weighing more than 14,000 tonnes. It was towed 160 kms (100 miles) from Scotland and launched from a 152 metre (500 ft) long barge. It was then uprighted, through controlled ballasting, by flooding huge steel bottles which form the bottom section of each leg.

Once the jacket was in position, piles were set 116 metres (380 ft) into the sea bed. This foundation provides a reliable support in seas of up to 29 metres (96 ft). Construction of the complete platform took in the region of two years from the placing of orders.

The platform can accommodate up to 36 wells to produce an oil flow at peak in excess of 300,000 barrels per day. Sophisticated equipment then controls and regulates the flow of oil from the field via the pipeline to an oil terminal in Orkney. The platform is equipped to treat sea water and inject it under pressure at rates of over 300,000 barrels per day. This is in order to supplement the natural pressure and ensure efficient recovery. The production equipment includes vessels for oil and gas separation, gas compressors, pipeline pumps, as well as the equipment necessary to provide life support, safety and emergency personnel protection.

1 drilling rig
2 flare boom
3 helicopter decks
4 living quarters
5 deck support frame
6 steel jacket
7 well conductors

Concrete platforms

Though oil rigs and platforms are traditionally constructed from steel there are a number of advantages in concrete structures. In the first place, no piling is needed, as the force of gravity enables the platform to rest in a stable position on the sea bed. Another important advantage is that much of a concrete platform can be made hollow, allowing space for the storing of crude oil, which is not possible with a steel structure. In very bad weather conditions – which often occur in the North Sea, for example – tankers are unable to approach oil platforms because of the danger of collision. On steel platforms there are no storage facilities for the crude oil, and as shutting off the flow is not advisable, other means of storage have to be provided near by.

Two further advantages of concrete platforms are the speed with which they can be installed –
much faster than with steel – and the fact that the whole platform can be towed to the oil field and positioned in one operation.

A notable example of a concrete oil platform is one designed by Mobil for their Beryl oil field (see page 24), and built at Stavanger in Norway. The base is made up of 19 cylindrical concrete cells which provide the greater part of the platform's storage capacity of 900,000 barrels. Each cell is 20 metres (66 feet) in diameter and 50 metres (164 feet) high. To produce them a timber formwork was built and concrete poured into it. Once the concrete had set, the formwork was lifted out by hydraulic jacks.

After completion of the base, three concrete towers were constructed, each of them 90 metres (295 feet) high. A steel deck was then built and attached to the top of the concrete towers. Finally, the whole structure was floated out to the Beryl field, the concrete cells were filled with sea water, and the platform was lowered into the water to a depth of 120 metres (394 feet).

Steel skirts around the cells penetrated the sea bed to hold the base permanently in position.

The concrete oil platform, Beryl A. How it was built is described on the next pages.

A concrete platform almost ready to be towed out to the oil field. The deck modules are still being constructed.

Concrete platforms are built in three main stages:

Stage one
This involves the excavation of a shallow basin, lower than sea level. The basin is dug close to the shore and is separated from the sea by either a natural earth bank or a purpose-built dock gate. Within this 'dry dock' the base of the platform and the vertical walls are built. A buoyant 'tray' is formed, on which the whole structure will eventually float.

The dock is in effect a self-contained construction site which may have its own railway siding, bulk storage facilities, and quayside. It may also be close to a quarry from which sand and gravel can be obtained. The dock will also have facilities for steel bending and concrete mixing. In one concrete platform alone over 150,000 tonnes of pre-stressed concrete, sand, gravel, cement, water and reinforced steel were used.

Stage two
Once the base of the structure is complete, the **dry dock** is flooded and the base is towed to a **wet dock** site. At the wet dock the structure is anchored and the vertical walls are finished. Sometimes a breakwater structure is also added. After two or three months the base is ready, with its legs attached.

Stage three
The platform is now moved to a deep water site, where the whole structure is sunk so that the deck modules can be added. The waters off the west coasts of Norway and Scotland are ideal places for these concrete platform sites, whereas steel platforms are generally constructed on the east coast of Scotland close to the North Sea oil fields.

The base is built onshore close to deep water so that it can be floated out when complete.

Building a concrete platform
1 The base of the platform is constructed in a dry dock which is then flooded.
2 The base is floated into deeper water.
3–5 The hollow concrete columns are constructed.

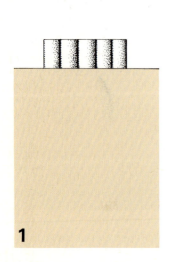

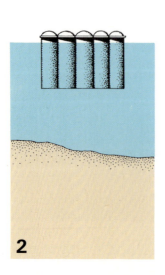

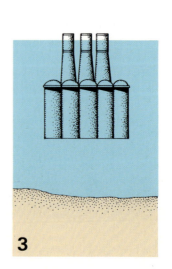

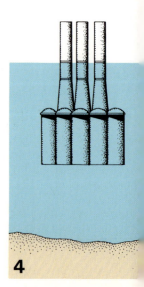

1

2

3

4

As with steel, concrete platforms must be designed to withstand the force of winds, waves and underwater pressure, as well as the weight of the basic structure and deck. All these stresses must be transmitted by the walls and columns to the base of the platform and then into the sea bed. If the soil layers of the sea bed are weak, a 'skirt' may have to be added to the structure which can be pressed down into the soil to strengthen its position.

The columns – here seen just above the water surface – are constructed and the deck modules are brought into position.

The whole platform is floated and towed out to the oil field by tugs.

6 The beginning of the deck modules are built on.
7 The platform is towed to the oil field.
8 The platform is positioned on the sea bed and the final elements built on to the deck.

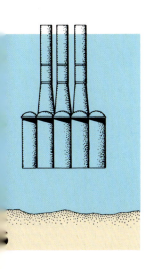

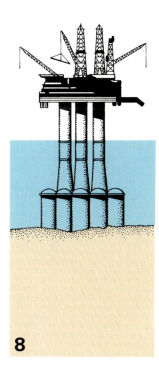

6

7

8

19

Float-out

Once the graving dock is flooded the jacket section can be towed out on its way to the oil field.

When the steel jacket has been completed, buoyancy tanks are attached to its base. The graving dock is then flooded and the jacket is towed out to the oil field by tugs. Obviously this operation has to be carried out in suitable weather conditions.

In order for it to be positioned on the sea bed the jacket has to be moved from its side to an upright position. First the ballast tanks are flooded, and the structure comes to rest on its side on the surface. Then by further computer-controlled flooding, the jacket is swung to a vertical position, still floating above the sea bed. The tugs make final adjustments to the positioning, and gradually the remaining tanks are flooded, so that the jacket sinks to the sea bed.

Once in position, the piles are hammered into place, with the jacket forming the base structure for the platform. The steel frame which will support the various modules forming the main part of the platform is then fixed to the top of the jacket with the help of huge cranes. This phase of the operation may take two to three months.

Float-out
1 The Magnus jacket towed out on a specially-built barge
2 The jacket is removed from the barge
3 The jacket lies in a horizontal position
4 It is moved to a vertical position
5 The jacket is positioned over the well
6 The platform rests on the sea bed
7 Piles secure the platform to the sea bed

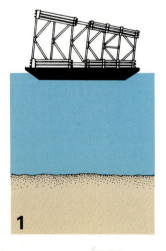

1

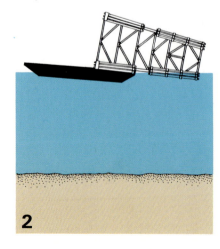

2

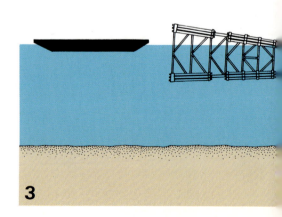

3

The jacket arrives above the oil field. The next step is to change its horizontal position to a vertical one.

Once over the oil field computers control the roll and final vertical positioning of the jacket. An anxious moment for those who have worked for years on the structure.

With the jacket in position and fixed to the sea bed work can begin on the installation of the deck modules.

The largest single-piece steel structure so far designed for the North Sea is BP's Magnus platform, which weighs over 34,000 tonnes. It consists of 17 modules built in different fabrication yards which provide:

    accommodation space for 200 people
    processing equipment
    a power plant
    a gas liquid recovery system
    water injection equipment.

The structure also has to support the drilling derrick, a 98-metre (320-ft) flare tower, a radio mast and three cranes.

The Magnus platform is eight storeys high and when the field is at peak production it will be capable of processing 12,000 barrels of crude oil and about 60 million cubic feet of gas *every day*.

An underwater hammer driving a pile in to secure one leg of the jacket to the sea bed.

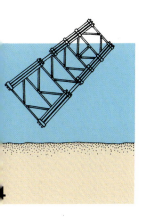

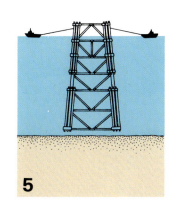

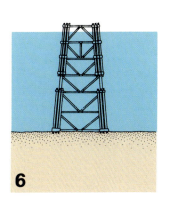

Modules

An oil production platform has three principal functions: (1) drilling, (2) controlling the flow of oil, and (3) providing all the necessary support facilities. The equipment and back-up services to fulfil these functions must all be housed on that part of the production platform which is above the surface of the sea.

A major oil field covers a vast area and it would not make economic sense for each platform to drill only one well, so **directional drilling** is employed. By this method one platform can drill up to 30 wells. The bit drills vertically for a given distance and is then moved on to another point and slightly angled, so that one platform with 30 wells can cover a vast area around the main vertical well.

Geological data about the field enable the oilmen to estimate how many wells are required and at what depth. This provides an indication of the amount of drilling equipment and the number and size of derricks which have to be housed in the production platform.

Once the wells have been drilled, the flow of oil must be controlled. Oil and gas have to be separated, which requires special machinery. An enormous amount of power is used to operate all the equipment on the platform, so the necessary plant has to be installed.

At first, the oil may flow from the field under its own pressure but as time goes on it may be necessary to inject water or gas back into the reservoir to keep up the pressure. Here again, specialised machinery is required.

Finally there are accommodation modules. Up to 200 men may live on a platform and they need reasonably comfortable cabins, leisure facilities,

The scale of operations is illustrated by this hook from one of the cranes used to install deck modules on to a production platform.

Building the deck and platform

1 The deck support frame is hoisted into position on the jacket.
2–3 Deck modules to hold production facilities are installed.
4 The platform – complete with two drilling derricks – is ready for operation.

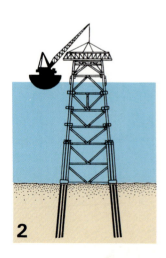
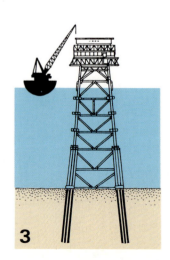
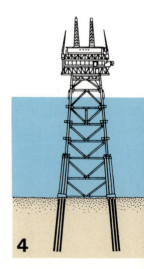

A crane vessel begins lifting deck modules on to the jacket section. Though calm, the weather has a grey North Sea appearance.

and good food, as well as communications equipment, and offices. The platforms have been compared to modern high rise office blocks where the cost of each square foot is extremely high and space is very limited. The task facing the designers is to fit all the necessary parts together so that the best possible use is made of the space available.

One of the major problems on an oil platform is noise, so the living and leisure modules are built as far away as possible from the working parts, such as the area around the derrick. It would also be impractical to put all the heavy machinery in one place, thus creating an imbalance in the overall load. Both these factors have to be carefully considered at the design stage. Even more important is the need for safety. Access routes have to be planned and hazardous machinery kept away from accommodation areas; all equipment must be spark-free to avoid danger from gas process

units; and excess gas has to be flared on special stacks well away from places that might suffer heat damage.

Heavy materials are delivered to the platforms by supply ship, but the main means of transport for taking men and light equipment to and from the shore are helicopters. All platforms have one, or sometimes two, helicopter landing decks, equipped with radio and fuel supplies, lights and planned overshoot paths.

To keep track of the movement of personnel to and from the shore, and also between platforms, at least one oil company – BP – has devised a computer-operated system. Each crew member has an identity card, details of which are fed into a computer whenever he leaves or arrives at a BP platform. In this way the Company knows the whereabouts of all staff on the platform. In the unlikely event of an accident, this system is extremely useful in ensuring that everyone is safe.

Deck modules (storage, flare tower, etc) being taken by barge to the jacket.

23

Directional drilling

Directional drilling allows 30 or more wells to be drilled from a single platform. The wells splay out so that a large area of the oil field can be covered. This cross-section shows a concrete platform, Beryl A, which operates in 120 metres (394 feet) of water. The oil field is about 3000 metres (1.86 miles) below the platform but directional drilling means that some wells are about 5000 metres (3 miles) from the platform. The produced oil is kept in the concrete storage tanks and goes by pipeline to the mooring and loading point about a mile away, where tankers can pump it on board. The map shows how two platforms, Beryl A and Beryl B, can cover the major part of an oil field using this technique. The circles are about 6 km (4 miles) across.

Beryl B

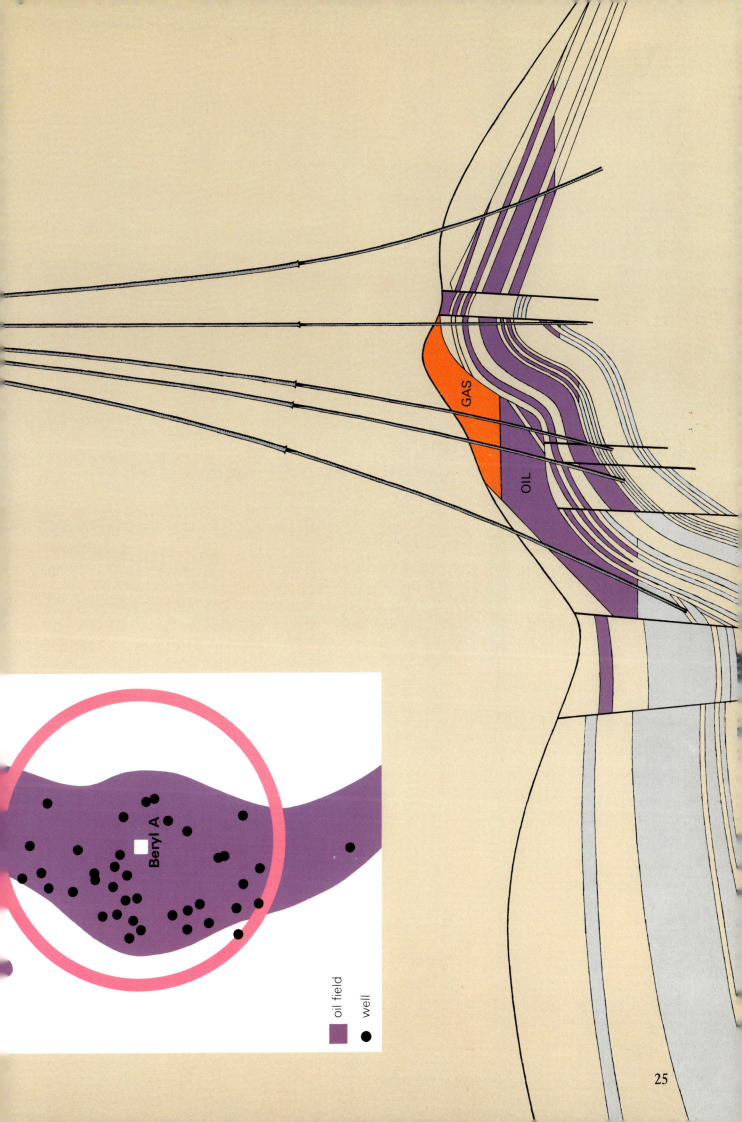

GAS

OIL

Beryl A

oil field

well

A pipe-laying barge. Lengths of pipe are welded together on board and then the pipe is lowered to the sea bed. The pipe can be seen at the end of the vessel where it goes into the sea and on to the sea bed.

The lengths of pipe are being welded together.

Here a steel cage is being made to reinforce the concrete coating on an underwater pipeline.

Pipelines

Since many offshore oil fields are a long way from land, provision has to be made for bringing the oil ashore from the platforms. There are two ways of doing this: by pipeline or by tanker.

On land, the problem is less complicated. For example, the Kirkuk oil fields in Northern Iran are 800 kilometres (497 miles) from the sea, and pipelines are the only practical way of moving large quantities of crude oil over such a long distance. In this and other remote, uninhabited areas where weather conditions are favourable, the pipes can be laid above the ground.

Providing **underwater pipelines** is a much more costly and difficult operation. Made from steel, the pipes have to be laid from specially designed barges, and the operation can be carried out only in fair weather. It can cost more than £1 million (about $1.4 million) to lay a mile of pipeline.

Underwater pipes are generally between 51 and 91 cms (20 and 36 inches) in diameter and are made up into 12-metre (39-foot) lengths. They are coated with a thick layer of anti-corrosive substance and an 8- to 10-cm (3- to 4-inch) layer of reinforced cement, which gives additional weight to the pipes and prevents them from buckling during the laying process. They are then welded together on the barges at sea.

Before they are laid, a trench has to be dug in the sea bed, and when they have been lowered into position they are inspected to make sure that there are no leakages.

Sullom Voe terminal in the Shetlands. Much North Sea oil is pumped to a land terminal to be taken on by tankers.

Because of the demand for pipelines the designers are always aware of the need for improvement, and new techniques are constantly being developed. The most recent one is the **spirally welded pipe**, which is made from steel strips wound in a spiral to the required diameter.

An offshore field is generally geared to producing a specific amount of oil each day, measured in **barrels** (159 litres, or 35 gallons). If a pipeline is used, the oil can flow continuously; it is pumped up to the production platform, passed straight into the pipeline and flows to the shore without being affected by adverse weather conditions.

The alternative method is by **tanker**, which because of sea movement and winds cannot moor alongside the production platforms. Mooring points therefore have to be provided, about a mile (1.6 km) away from the platforms. A short pipeline carries the oil from the platform to the mooring point, where it is taken on by the tanker. Once a tanker has been loaded, another takes its place – hours, or perhaps days, later.

With the tanker system the flow of oil cannot be continuous, so there have to be storage facilities at the mooring point (this, of course, is not necessary in the case of concrete platforms, which have their own storage capacity). The tanker-loading system only works well when weather conditions are good, and in the hostile environment of the North Sea there is greater reliance on pipelines, in spite of the high costs.

MATTHEW BOULTON
TECHNICAL COLLEGE
COLLEGE LIBRARY

A tanker taking on oil from a single-point mooring buoy. A drilling rig can be seen in the background.

Glossary

Anticline   The simplest type of oil reservoir – a dome-shaped structure capped with impervious rock. Most Middle East reservoirs are anticlines. Typically, they are about 30 miles long and 5 miles wide.

Blow-out preventer   A hydraulically operated device which is positioned at the well-head. It controls the pressure of the drilling-mud and, as its name suggests, prevents surges of oil breaking out of the well.

Cable-tool system   An early method of drilling. The bit was suspended by a length of wire. As the wire was jerked, the bit dug into the earth.

Crude oil   This term is generally used to describe oil that is found in its natural state underground. In the oil industry the term refers specifically to oil from which any gas has been removed but which has not passed through any other processes. When it does, it will be 'refined'.

Derrick   Originally made from wood, derricks are the familiar towers associated with the oil industry. Today they are made from steel. A derrick must be high enough to store at least three lengths of 30-foot (9-metre) drill-pipe. It must also be able to support the maximum amount of pipe required in drilling a particular well.

Directional drilling   A term used to describe drilling a number of wells from a single production platform. The first well is drilled vertically. Further wells are drilled at a slight angle. As the depth of the wells increases, the distance from the vertical becomes greater. In this way a single platform can produce enough wells to cover a large area of an oil field.

Diving   Divers play an important role in servicing and maintaining offshore structures. This diving bell is operating from ESV 'Iolair'.

Drill-bit   The drill-bit is the tool that actually penetrates the rock in the earth's surface. Many drill-bits have hard teeth to help bore into rock. Some modern bits are made from commercial diamonds. A hole through the centre of the bit and the grooves around its head allow drilling-mud to flow down to the rock and then back up to the surface.

Drilling-mud   This is a fluid which cools and lubricates the drill-bit, brings bits of rock to the surface, and prevents the walls of the well caving in. It is an extremely important part of drilling and requires the work of specialists to attain the right chemical ingredients.

Dynamically positioned drillship   By using thruster propellers controlled by computers, a drill ship can be held over a specific point without anchors. Constant firing of the correct motors maintains the vessel in the same position.

Dry dock   A large dock big enough to hold a vessel – such as a semi-submersible – while it is being constructed. Dry docks are generally used for repairs which necessitate working under the hull of a vessel.

Exploration rig   A floating structure which drills exploration holes, in the search for oil. There are many types of exploration rig, the most modern being the semi-submersible.

Flarestack   A high tower which carries unwanted gas away from the platform. The gas is then burnt off.

Graving dock   A large area of enclosed land at the edge of the sea used for the construction of steel 'jackets' for production platforms. When construction is complete, specially designed gates are opened to flood the dock. The jacket can then be floated out and towed to the oil field.

Gravity structure   A structure, such as a concrete platform, which is held in place by its own weight – or gravity.

Grouting   A method of sealing a hole. When piles are driven into the sea bed to hold a production platform in position, the holes are filled with cement grouting.

Gusher   An uncontrolled outburst of oil and gas which in the early days of drilling could cause a lot of damage. A stream of black oil would spray high into the air, often throwing up the drill-pipe and derrick. Such accidents are most unlikely today, with the introduction of valves and blow-out preventers.

Impermeable   Oil and water 'migrate', or move upward, through permeable rocks. Permeable rocks include limestone and sandstone which have tiny air spaces between the grains that make up the rock. However, their flow is halted by impermeable rock, such as granite and marble.

Jacket   The tubular steel structure which stands on the sea bed and supports the deck modules of a steel production platform. The jacket is built on its side in a graving dock and then floated out (sometimes on a barge) to the oil field. It is then tipped upright under computer control.

Metal fatigue   Any metal structures (oil rigs, cars, aeroplanes) are subject to constant stresses or 'fatigue'. These may come from their own weight or from environmental forces such as winds and seas.

Piled structure   Some structures, such as steel production platforms, are fixed in position with long pieces of steel called 'piles', which are hammered

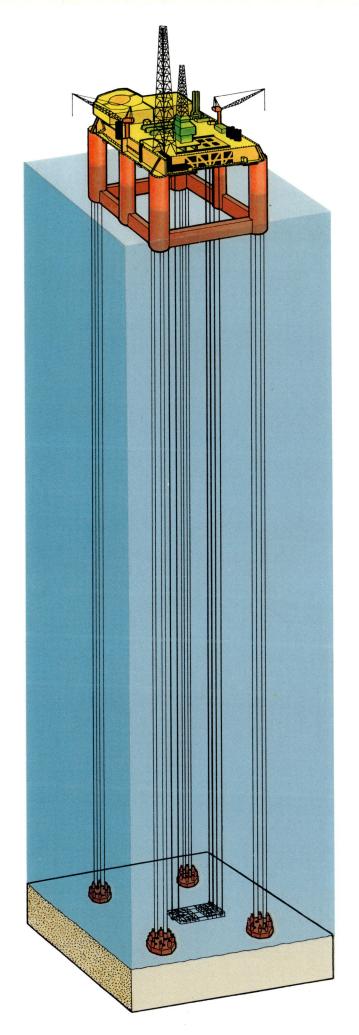

through the structure and into the sea bed. The piles ensure that the structure will remain secured to the sea bed.

Pontoon A hollow metal structure used to support a vessel such as a semi-submersible. The pontoons help to keep such structures stable.

Production platform The structure – either steel or concrete – which stands on the sea bed over an oil field. It is installed once an oil field has been discovered, and it carries all the equipment necessary to produce oil and gas from an oil field. Further wells are drilled from such a platform, and the constant flow of oil and gas is maintained.

Riser system The system of pipes which allows gas or oil to flow up to the surface.

Rotary drilling The system which superseded cable-tool drilling. A rotating table turns the drill-pipe which in turn rotates the drill-bit.

Rotating table A circular piece of steel with a square hole at its centre. It is rotated horizontally, and turns the drill-pipe and bit.

Skirt The structure at the base of a concrete production platform – so-called because it looks like a skirt.

Support vessels Specially built vessels provide safety cover for oil platforms. An example is BP's 'Iolair' which provides a fire-fighting capability, emergency quarters, diving facilities, and a hospital as well as a routine maintenance base, and helicopter operations. Here, fire-fighting equipment is being used.

Tethered platforms Also known as Tension Leg Platforms (left). These are essentially buoyant production platforms which do away with the more familiar steel jacket. High-tensile steel rods allow lateral but not vertical movement. This new development can be used in any depth of water and cuts the cost of conventional platforms.

Turbo-drilling A more sophisticated form of rotary drilling in which a turbine is positioned just above the drill-bit. The turbine is powered by the drilling-mud which is pumped under greater pressure than usual. This means that the rotary table need not move at all, though turning it slowly does improve drilling performance.

Wet dock This is the usual kind of dock, which vessels can approach through water.

The tethered platform

People in the oil industry

Geologists, Geophysicists, Geochemists locate likely oil-bearing strata and then pinpoint areas to be drilled

Surveyors survey and map field

Drilling engineers supervise drilling from initial planning to reporting the results

Petroleum engineers monitor operations at well site and interpret results

Production engineers decide on the economic viability of well site, decide what equipment will be needed, then supervise once production has started

Once it has been agreed to go ahead, tenders are sent out for equipment and services. The oil industry, perhaps more than any other, employs a large number of outside contractors for both project management and manual duties.

Who builds oil rigs?

Design engineers design structures suitable for sea and weather conditions

Project managers co-ordinate and supervise work and meet target dates

Production platforms

Welders	Fitters
Fabricators	Electricians
Riggers	Instrument technicians and fitters
Scaffolders	Pipe fitters
Plant operators	Pipe welders
Millwrights	Engineers

Hooking up modules on site

Engineers	Radio operators
Administrative team	Mechanics
Construction workers	Instrument technicians

Drilling personnel

Toolpushers	Derrickmen
Drillers (supervisors)	Rig crewmen
Assistant drillers	Roustabouts
(rig crew foremen)	Crane operators

The heart of a modern oil platform looks like the bridge of a conventional vessel.

Safety is vital in the hazardous environment of the North Sea. Here lifeboat drill is practised.

Hard work in the cold North Sea deserves warm accommodation and good food. Both are provided in plenty.

Computers are now an integral part of the oil industry. They are used in the design of new oil rigs and are particularly useful in calculating areas of maximum stress so that construction can meet the highest safety standards.

Important dates

1840 Brine (salt) well drilled to a depth of over 305 metres (1000 feet), in USA
1859 'Colonel' Drake drills a brine well in Titusville, Pennsylvania, USA, and finds oil. This is the beginning of the oil industry
1884 Oil discovered in the Rocky Mountains, USA
1890 Royal Dutch Company formed
1897 Shell Transport and Trading Company formed
1901 Spindletop field, Texas, USA, discovered by the new rotary method of drilling
1908 First major oil discovery in Mexico
1909 Rolling cutter rock-bit invented
1917 Oil discovered in Oklahoma City, USA
1918 World's deepest well stands at 2250 metres (7386 feet)
1920s First offshore drilling in swamps of Louisiana, USA. Texas becomes a major producer
1927 Introduction of self-cleaning cutters on the rock-bit
1937 Natural gas discovered at Eskdale, Yorkshire
1939 First major oil field discovered at Eakring, near Nottingham
1958 Oil discovered at Gainsborough, Lincolnshire
1959 Oil discovered at Kimmeridge, Dorset
1961 North Sea gas discovered at Slochteren, Groningen, in the Netherlands. One of the world's largest gas fields
1964 Continental Shelf Act drafted and passed. Exploration licences granted in UK sector of North Sea
1965 BP discover West Sole gas field in the North Sea
1967 First gas piped ashore from West Sole to Easington, Yorkshire
1969 Montrose oil field discovered by Amoco in the North Sea. Oil discovered in Alaska by BP
1970 Norwegians discover Ekofisk oil field in the North Sea. BP discover the first major oil field in the UK sector – Forties
1971 Expro discover the Auk oil field in the North Sea. Hamilton Brothers Oil Co discover Argyll oil field
1972 Expro discover Brent and Cormorant in the North Sea. Mobil discover Beryl oil field
1973 Piper (Occidental)
Maureen, Dunlin (Expro) } oil fields discovered
Heather (Unocal)   in the North Sea
Thistle (Britoil)
Hutton (Conoco)
1974 North Sea Ninian oil field discovered. Claymore and Buchan discovered.
1977 Trans-Alaskan pipeline begins operating
1983 BP signs concession agreement to drill in Chinese offshore areas

Index

Acknowledgements

Illustration credits
Photographs: British Petroleum Company Limited 2, 5 (right), 7, 8, 12 (top), 13, 20, 21, 22, 23, 26, 27 (bottom), 28 (top); British Shipbuilders 3, 9, 11, 27 (top); Cleveland Redpath Engineering Holdings Limited 10; Mobil North Sea Limited 5 (left), 12 (bottom), 16, 18, 19, 30 (second bottom and bottom); Occidental Oil Britain, Inc 28 (bottom), 30 (second top), 31; Wimpey Group Services 17, 30 (top).

Diagrams and drawings: Ray Burrows 6, 8, 10, 11, 18/19, 20/21, 22, 24/25, 29; Gillian Newing 4, 5; Occidental Oil Britain, Inc 14/15.

MATTHEW BOULTON
TECHNICAL COLLEGE
COLLEGE LIBRARY

First published in 1985
by Faber and Faber Limited
3 Queen Square, London WC1N 3AU

Typeset by Phoenix Photosetting, Chatham, Kent
Origination by Culver Graphics, London
Printed and bound in Belgium by
Henri Proost & Cie PVBA
All rights reserved

© Threshold Books Limited, 1985

The How It Is Made series was conceived, designed and produced by Threshold Books Limited
661 Fulham Road, London SW6 5PZ

General Editor: Barbara Cooper

No part of this publication may be reproduced, stored in a retrieval system, or transmitted, in any form or by any means, electronic or otherwise, without written permission of the publisher.

British Library Cataloguing in Publication Data

Lynch, Michael
    Oil rigs.—(How it is made)
    1. Oil well drilling, Submarine—Juvenile literature
    I. Title   II. Series
    622'.3382   TN 871.3
    ISBN 0–571–13414–9